In the Name of Allah the Gracious, the Merciful

Copyright © 2021 by Lantern Publications

All rights reserved. No part of this publication may be reproduced, distributed, or transmitted in any form or by any means, including photocopying, recording, or other electronic or mechanical methods, without the prior written permission of the publisher, except in the case of brief quotations embodied in critical reviews and certain other noncommercial uses permitted by copyright law. For permission requests, write to the publisher, addressed "Attention: - Permissions (Noah  Builds a Lifesaving Ship)," at the email address below.

Lantern Publications
info@lanternpublications.com
www.lanternkids.com.au

A catalogue record for this book is available from the National Library of Australia

Ordering Information:

Quantity sales. Special discounts are available on quantity purchases by corporations, associations, and others. For details, contact the distributor at the address above.

Written by: Abbass Noureddin | **Illustrated by:** Tahera Amini |
Translated by: Amal Abdallah | **Edited by:** Dr Abidali Mohamedali

ISBN- 978-1-922583-17-8
Abbreviations used in this book:
()- Alayhis Salaam – May peace be upon him.

First Edition

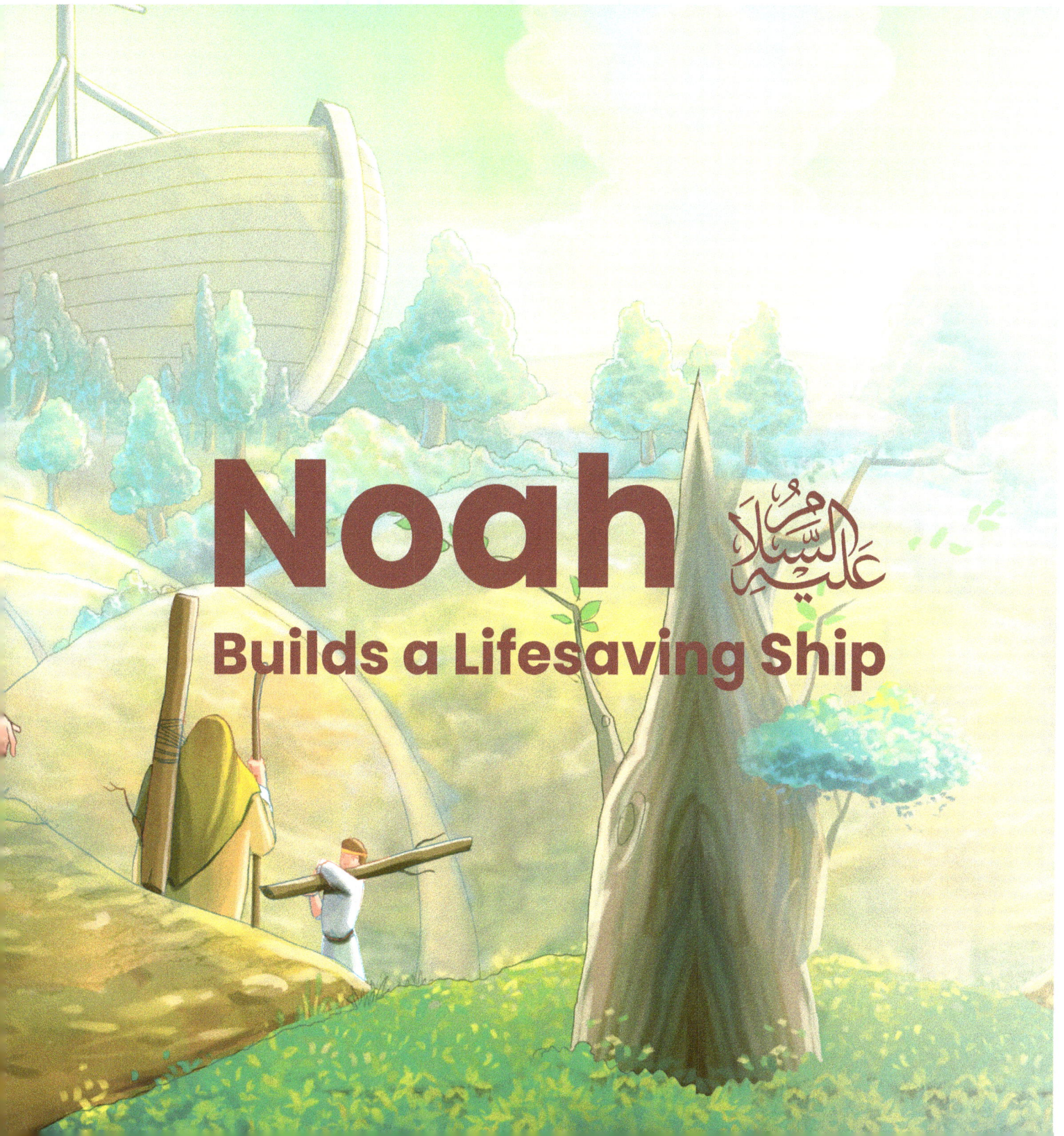

The lofty garden is every man's dream. If man stays true to this dream and follows it, it will become true.

Adam ﷺ came with a vow from God to all mankind. It stated that if humans seek reform and follow God's vicegerent¹, they will reach that garden.

However, Satan was on the lookout.

---

1 Vicegerent: a person appointed to exercise all or some of the authority of another

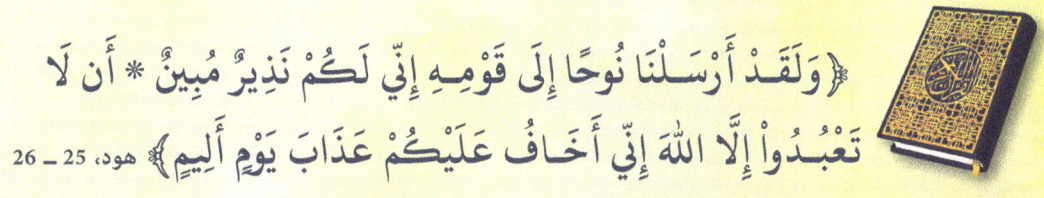

﴿وَلَقَدْ أَرْسَلْنَا نُوحًا إِلَىٰ قَوْمِهِ إِنِّي لَكُمْ نَذِيرٌ مُبِينٌ ۞ أَن لَّا تَعْبُدُوا إِلَّا اللَّهَ إِنِّي أَخَافُ عَلَيْكُمْ عَذَابَ يَوْمٍ أَلِيمٍ﴾ هود، 25 – 26

Certainly [it was with the same message that] We sent Noah to his people [to declare]: "Indeed I am a manifest warner to you. Worship none but Allah. Indeed I fear for you the punishment of a painful day."
Hud: 25, 26

Satan made many of Adam's ﷺ sons forget about that garden. So, they neglected God's vow.

However, before his death, Adam ﷺ passed God's plan and vow to his successor, to remind the people about it. Then Adam's ﷺ son passed the vow to his successor, and so on till it reached Noah ﷺ, who started reminding people of God's vow.

﴿قَالَ رَبِّ إِنِّي دَعَوْتُ قَوْمِي لَيْلًا وَنَهَارًا ۝ فَلَمْ يَزِدْهُمْ دُعَائِي إِلَّا فِرَارًا ۝ وَإِنِّي كُلَّمَا دَعَوْتُهُمْ لِتَغْفِرَ لَهُمْ جَعَلُوا أَصَابِعَهُمْ فِي آذَانِهِمْ وَاسْتَغْشَوْا ثِيَابَهُمْ وَأَصَرُّوا وَاسْتَكْبَرُوا اسْتِكْبَارًا﴾ نوح، 5 – 7

[After a time] He said, "My Lord, I have called my people night and day. but my call has only caused them to flee farther and farther away [from You]. And indeed, whenever I called unto them so that You might forgive them, they put their fingers into their ears, and wrapped themselves up in their garments [of sin]; and grew obstinate, and became [yet more] arrogant in their false pride." Noah: 5-7

When Noah ﷺ started calling people to God's plan, he discovered that they had stopped dreaming about the lofty garden. They cared for nothing but their present life, even though this made their lives miserable. Noah ﷺ told them that this world would not be reformed unless they carried out God's plan. "We need to transform this Earth into a ship that will carry us to our eternal residence," Noah ﷺ said, stating God's Plan.

﴿قَالَ نُوحٌ رَبِّ إِنَّهُمْ عَصَوْنِي وَاتَّبَعُوا مَن لَّمْ يَزِدْهُ مَالُهُ وَوَلَدُهُ إِلَّا خَسَارًا * وَمَكَرُوا مَكْرًا كُبَّارًا﴾ نوح، 21

Noah said, 'My Lord! They have disobeyed me, following someone whose wealth and children only add to his loss, and they have devised an outrageous plot." Noah: 21,22

Those who adored this life and forgot about the afterlife and paradise tried their best to stay in this world.

They thought that their fortunes would keep them alive, so they started piling up riches. The strong started robbing the weak until people were divided into two classes: the strong, who owned a lot of money, and the weak, who became poor.

﴿وَقَالُوا لَا تَذَرُنَّ ءَالِهَتَكُمْ وَلَا تَذَرُنَّ وَدًّا وَلَا سُوَاعًا وَلَا يَغُوثَ وَيَعُوقَ وَنَسْرًا﴾ نوح، 23

And they said, "Do not abandon your gods.; do not give up Wadd, nor Suwa', nor Yaghuth, and Ya'uq, and Nassr." Noah:23

The rich were afraid that the poor might unite and rebel against them, so they sought to control them through deception. They built idols and told the poor that those idols gave them strength.

"If you worship these gods, they will give you strength, and if you offer them money, they will reward you with more, but if you disobey them, they will punish you!" the rich told the poor.

The poor fell for that trick. The rich started piling up the offerings that the poor made to the idols, which made them richer!

﴿وَقَدْ أَضَلُّوا كَثِيرًا وَلَا تَزِدِ الظَّالِمِينَ إِلَّا ضَلَالًا﴾ نوح، 24

And already they have led many astray. Do not increase the wrongdoers in anything but error."
Noah:24

The rich grew stronger. They dominated the poor and demanded total obedience from them. They ordered the poor to gather all the riches in the land. To dig out all the gold and silver, the poor had to plunder the land. Thus, havoc spread everywhere.

﴿قَالُواْ يَا نُوحُ قَدْ جَادَلْتَنَا فَأَكْثَرْتَ جِدَالَنَا فَأْتِنَا بِمَا تَعِدُنَا إِن كُنتَ مِنَ الصَّادِقِينَ * قَالَ إِنَّمَا يَأْتِيكُم بِهِ اللَّهُ إِن شَاءَ وَمَا أَنتُم بِمُعْجِزِينَ﴾ نوح، 32 _ 33

They said, "O Noah, you have argued with us and argued a great deal. Now bring upon us what you threaten us with if you are truthful." Hud:32

God -the Almighty- sent his prophet Noah ﷺ to warn the people. Noah said," If you ruin the earth, there will be trouble and disasters, and torture will be sent down on the tyrants!"

However, the rich grew more and more greedy. They continued to turn their back to God's vow and to the dream of the lofty garden.

﴿ثُمَّ إِنِّي دَعَوْتُهُمْ جِهَارًا ۝ ثُمَّ إِنِّي أَعْلَنتُ لَهُمْ وَأَسْرَرْتُ لَهُمْ إِسْرَارًا﴾ نوح، 8 ـ 9

﴿وَأُوحِيَ إِلَىٰ نُوحٍ أَنَّهُ لَن يُؤْمِنَ مِن قَوْمِكَ إِلَّا مَن قَدْ آمَنَ فَلَا تَبْتَئِسْ بِمَا كَانُوا يَفْعَلُونَ ۝ وَاصْنَعِ الْفُلْكَ بِأَعْيُنِنَا وَوَحْيِنَا وَلَا تُخَاطِبْنِي فِي الَّذِينَ ظَلَمُوا إِنَّهُم مُّغْرَقُونَ﴾ هود، 36 ـ 37

"Again I summoned them aloud. and again appealed to them publicly and confided with them privately." Noah:8-9

And it was revealed to Noah: "None of your people will believe, except those who have already have faith, so do not grieve over what they used to do. Build the ark before Our eyes and by Our revelation, and do not plead with Me for those who are wrongdoers: they shall indeed be drowned." Hud:36-37

Noah ﷺ called his people secretly and openly to God's plan for hundreds of years and reminded them of God's vow. However, it was no use. Only a few answered his call. The rest continued to sabotage the earth. So, God told His prophet that a disaster would soon strike and that he had to build a lifesaving ship.

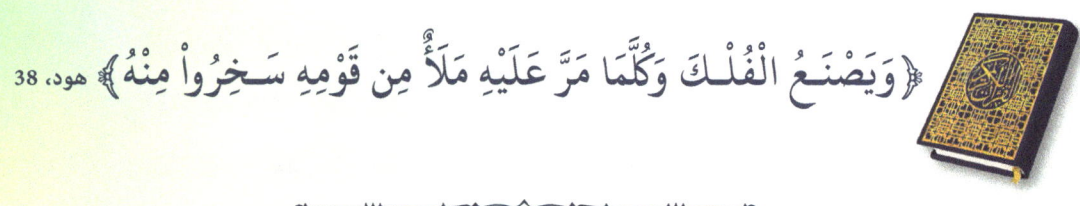

﴿وَيَصْنَعُ الْفُلْكَ وَكُلَّمَا مَرَّ عَلَيْهِ مَلَأٌ مِن قَوْمِهِ سَخِرُوا۟ مِنْهُ﴾ هود، 38

As he was building the ark, whenever the elders of his people passed by him, they would make fun of him. He [Noah] said, "If you ridicule us [today], we shall ridicule you [tomorrow] just as you ridicule us [now]"
Hud:38

Noah ﷺ started building the ark that would carry the believers and the animals. God wanted the people to see the ark so that they would repent and believe. However, the arrogant started making fun of Noah ﷺ. They told the people, "Look at that crazy man building a ship so far from water!"

﴿ حَتَّىٰ إِذَا جَاءَ أَمْرُنَا وَفَارَ التَّنُّورُ قُلْنَا احْمِلْ فِيهَا مِن كُلٍّ زَوْجَيْنِ اثْنَيْنِ وَأَهْلَكَ إِلَّا مَن سَبَقَ عَلَيْهِ الْقَوْلُ وَمَنْ آمَنَ وَمَا آمَنَ مَعَهُ إِلَّا قَلِيلٌ * وَقَالَ ارْكَبُوا فِيهَا بِسْمِ اللَّهِ مَجْرَاهَا وَمُرْسَاهَا إِنَّ رَبِّي لَغَفُورٌ رَحِيمٌ ﴾ هود، 40 – 41

﴿ وَقِيلَ يَا أَرْضُ ابْلَعِي مَاءَكِ وَيَا سَمَاءُ أَقْلِعِي وَغِيضَ الْمَاءُ وَقُضِيَ الْأَمْرُ وَاسْتَوَتْ عَلَى الْجُودِيِّ وَقِيلَ بُعْدًا لِلْقَوْمِ الظَّالِمِينَ ﴾ هود، 44

[And so it went on] till, when Our judgment came to pass, and waters gushed forth in torrents over the face of the earth, We said [to Noah]: "Place on board of this [ark] one pair of each [kind of animal] of either sex, as well as your family -except those on whom [Our] sentence has already been passed -and all [others] who believe!"-for, only a few shared his faith, So he said [to his followers]: "Embark in this [ship]! In the name of God, be it's run, and it's riding at anchor! Behold, my. Sustainer is indeed much-forgiving, all-merciful!" Hud:40, 41

And the word was spoken: "O earth, swallow up thy waters! And, O sky, stop [your rain]!" The waters sank into the earth, and the will [of God] was done, and the ark came to rest on Mount Judi, and the word was spoken: "Away with the wicked people!" Hud:44

"Water will pour out of a furnace!" that was the sign of God's rage. Once the sign came true, the believers rushed into the ark carrying with them a pair of each kind of animal in the area. They had to preserve the animals as well as reform the earth. God wanted the believers to start life all over again in a land free of corruption. For that reason, there was a great flood.

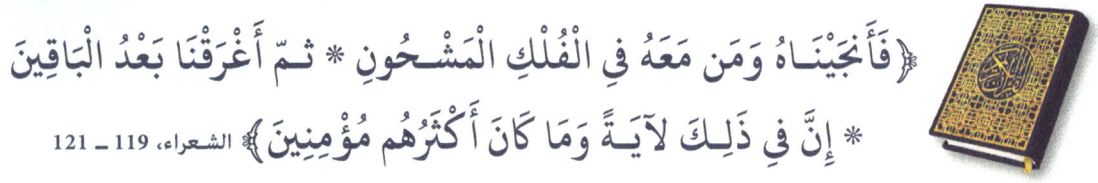

﴿ فَأَنجَيْنَاهُ وَمَن مَّعَهُ فِي الْفُلْكِ الْمَشْحُونِ ۞ ثُمَّ أَغْرَقْنَا بَعْدُ الْبَاقِينَ ۞ إِنَّ فِي ذَٰلِكَ لَآيَةً ۖ وَمَا كَانَ أَكْثَرُهُم مُّؤْمِنِينَ ﴾ الشعراء، 119 - 121

"And so, We saved him and those [who were] with him in the fully-laden ark. And then We caused those who stayed behind to drown. In this [story], behold, there is a message [for men], even though most of them will not believe [in it]." Poets:119-121

When the believers saw the flood and saw how the non-believers perished, they got to understand God's greatness and omnipotence.

It became clear that God aids His prophets and aids anyone who follows their lead and works to fulfil His plan, even after hundreds of years!

MORE READING

Arastu .R., *Gods Emissaries – From Adam to Jesus* (2019), Imam Mahdi Association of Marjaeya (IMAM)- A brilliant book to get more details on the life of Prophet Noah ﷺ

Majlisi, Baqir Al-, *Hayat Al-Qulub, Vol. 1, Stories of the Prophets,* This book is one of the most significant contributions of Allama Majlisi and comes in 3 volumes. It is available online from al-islam.org

www.ingramcontent.com/pod-product-compliance
Lightning Source LLC
Chambersburg PA
CBHW051251110526
44588CB00025B/2956